# Coloring and Tracing

## Meimei---A Beautiful Fish 美美---一条美丽的鱼

written and illustrated by Yue Chen

# Dedication

I dedicate this book to YOU! Thanks for supporting *MeimeiStory* book series! Hope you enjoy tracing and coloring this book.

black / white
hēi sè  bái sè
黑色 / 白色

5

| 丨 | 冂 | 冂 | 罒 | 罒 | 罒 |
|---|---|---|---|---|---|

| 丿 | 勹 | 勹 | 勹 | 色 | 色 |
|---|---|---|---|---|---|

| 里 | 里 | 黑 | 黑 | 黑 | 黑 |
|---|---|---|---|---|---|

黑 色

白 ＇ ｀ ｒ 白 白

色 ＇ ｒ ｒ 各 名 色

red
hóng sè
红 色

8

乚 乡 纟 纟 红 红　　丿 ⺈ 刍 刍 刍 色

红 色

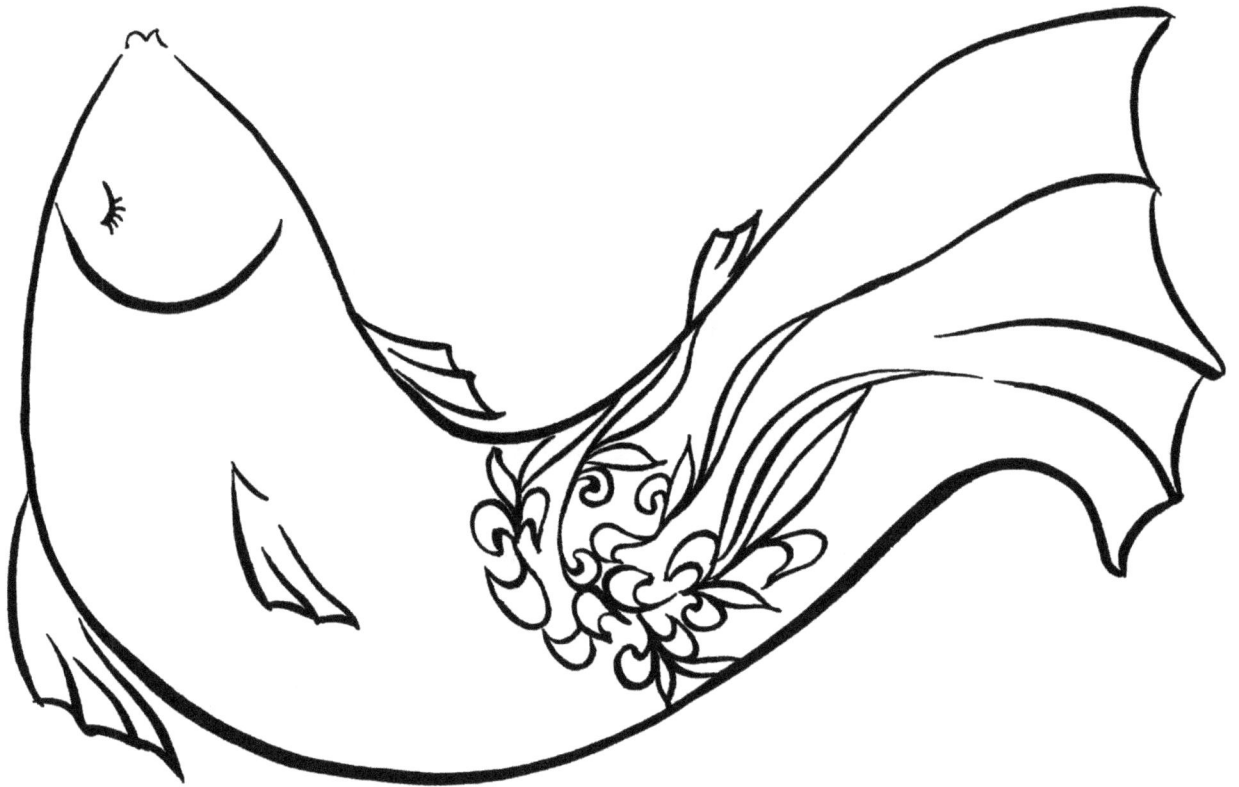

blue
lán sè
蓝色

10

| 一 | 十 | 艹 | 艹 | 艹 | 艹 |
|---|---|---|---|---|---|

| 艹 | 艹 | 艹 | 蓝 | 蓝 | 蓝 |
|---|---|---|---|---|---|

| 蓝 |
|---|

| ⺈ | ⺈ | 刍 | 刍 | 刍 | 色 |
|---|---|---|---|---|---|

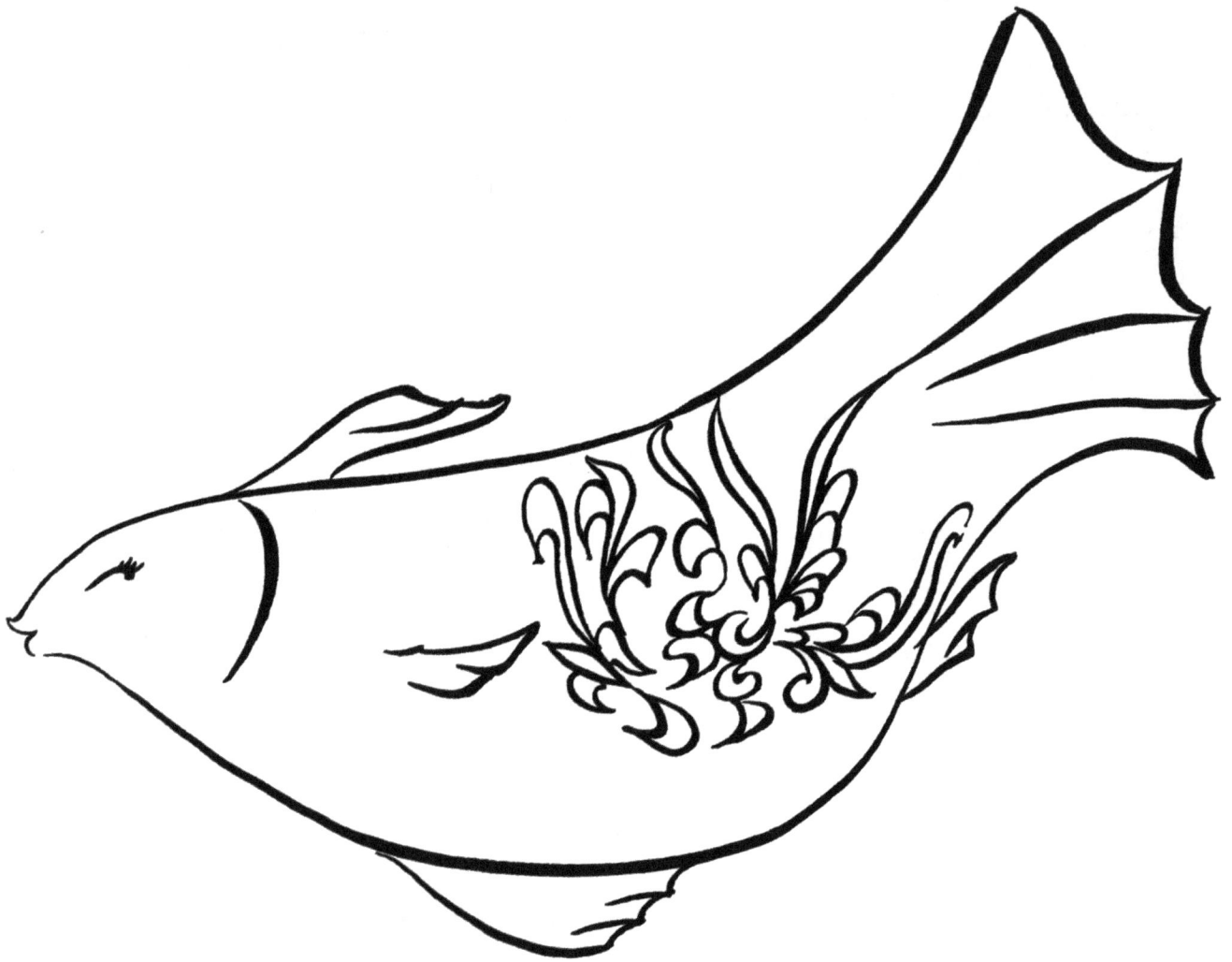

orange
chéng sè
橙 色

12

一 十 オ 才 木 杉 杉 松 桦 桦 椅 橙 橙 橙 橙

丿 ク 久 多 名 色

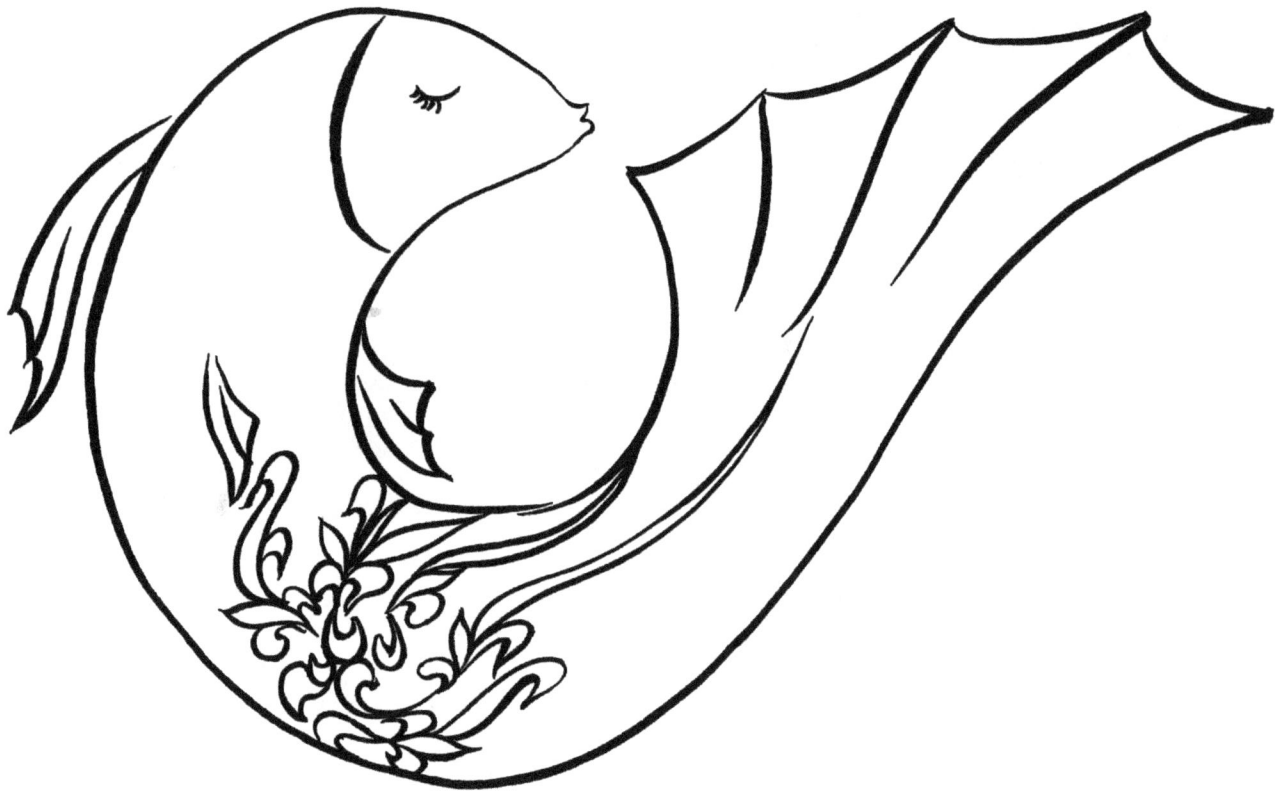

purple
zǐ sè
紫色

| 丨 | 卜 | 止 | 止 | 此 | 此 |
|---|---|---|---|---|---|

| 紫 | 紫 | 紫 | 紫 | 紫 | 紫 |
|---|---|---|---|---|---|

| ⺈ | ⺈ | 夕 | 负 | 负 | 色 |
|---|---|---|---|---|---|

green
lù sè
绿色

ㄑ ㄥ ㄠ 纟 纟 纡 纡 纡 绿 绿 绿

ノ ㄅ ㄅ ㄅ 色 色

绿色

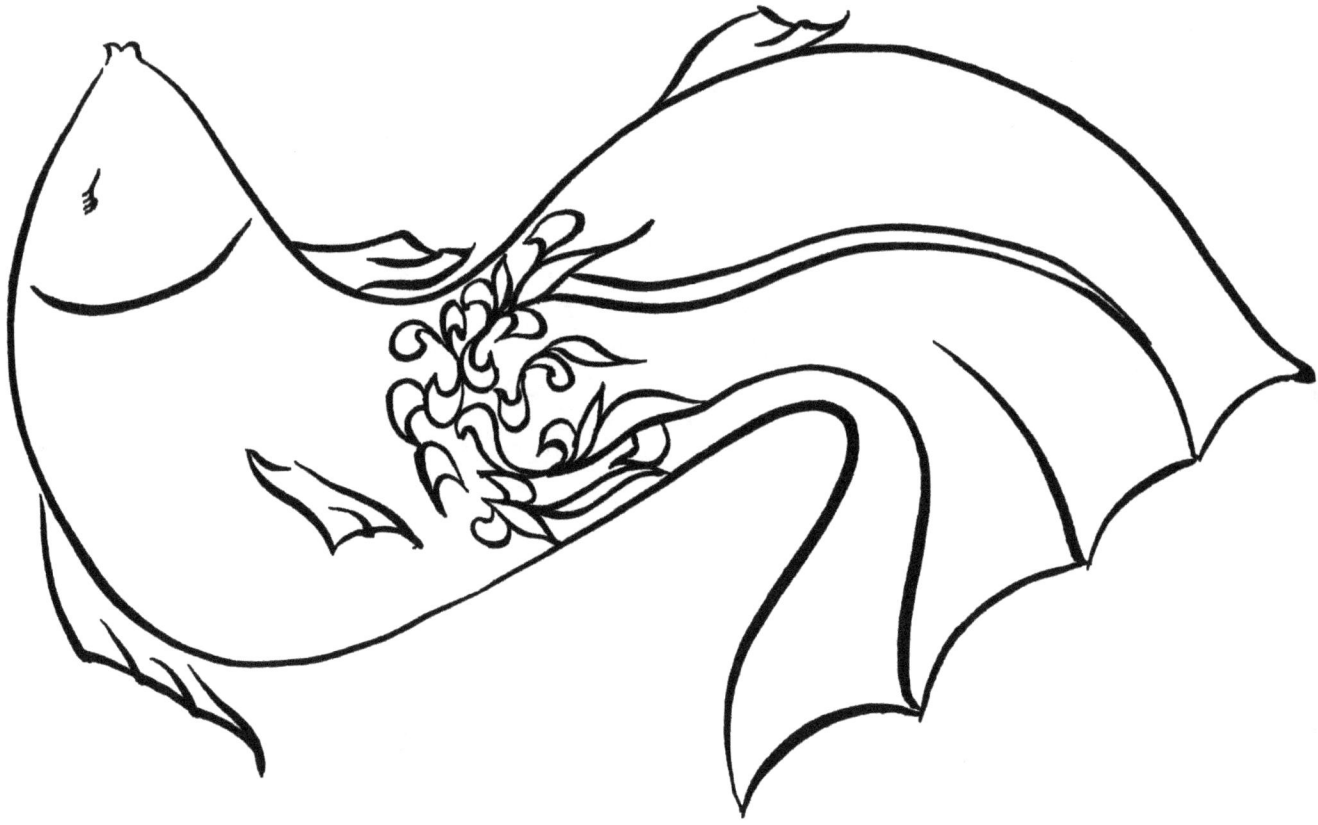

yellow
huáng sè
黄 色

18

| 一 | 十 | 艹 | 丗 | 芦 | 苫 |
|---|---|---|---|---|---|

| 苦 | 苗 | 苗 | 黄 | 黄 |
|---|---|---|---|---|

| ⺈ | ⺈ | ⺈ | 刍 | 刍 | 色 |
|---|---|---|---|---|---|

rainbow
cǎi sè
彩 色

**20**

一 厂 厂 厸 亚 平
采 采 彩 彩 彩

丿 ㇇ 冬 冬 色 色

Let's match them up!

| | |
|---|---|
| black | hóng sè |
| white | cǎi sè |
| red | zǐ sè |
| blue | chéng sè |
| yellow | bái sè |
| green | huáng sè |
| purple | lǜ sè |
| orange | lán sè |
| rainbow | hēi sè |

22

Let's match them up!

hóng sè

căi sè

zǐ sè

chéng sè

bái sè

huáng sè

lù sè

lán sè

hēi sè

橙色
红色
绿色
白色
彩色
蓝色
黄色
黑色
紫色

23

www.ingramcontent.com/pod-product-compliance
Lightning Source LLC
Chambersburg PA
CBHW080537030426
42337CB00023B/4778